HAWAI'I COOKS *with* COCONUT

Mutual Publishing

ISBN: 978-1-949307-72-6

Design by Jane Gillespie
First Printing, March 2025

Mutual Publishing, LLC
1215 Center Street, Suite 210
Honolulu, Hawai'i 96816
Ph: (808) 732-1709
Fax: (808) 734-4094
email: info@mutualpublishing.com
www.mutualpublishing.com

Printed in South Korea

CONTENTS

DESSERTS 77

INTRODUCTION

Coconuts have played an essential role in the culinary and cultural history of Hawaiʻi and across many other Pacific Islands. The niu, coconut palm, was one of the canoe plants that Polynesian voyagers brought with them to Hawaiʻi. Hawaiians used all parts of the tree. The coconut water, milk, meat, and oil were used for sustenance, while the husks and shells had functional uses such as fuel, craft-making, and storage.

Coconut is used in a variety of traditional Hawaiian dishes, often contributing a rich, creamy flavor to both sweet and savory recipes. One of the most popular desserts in Hawaiian cuisine is haupia, a pudding made from coconut milk, sugar, and arrowroot starch or cornstarch, giving it a firm, gelatinous consistency. Traditionally served as small cubes, haupia was often a ceremonial dish served during significant Hawaiian lūʻau. Today, it remains a popular dessert, served on its own or as part of layered desserts such as haupia pies, or even added as a topping for other sweets like cakes and tarts.

Beyond haupia, coconut appears in many other traditional Hawaiian dishes. For example, lau lau—a dish made from pork, fish, and vegetables wrapped in taro leaves—can be cooked with coconut milk, which adds a creaminess to the savory flavors. Coconut is also used in sauces, curries, and stews like squid lūʻau, enriching dishes with its distinctive flavor and nutritional benefits.

As immigrants from Japan, China, the Philippines, Korea, Portugal, and other countries came to Hawaiʻi, they brought their own culinary traditions. Coconut became an ingredient that bridged these diverse cultures. Filipino cuisine, introduced to Hawaiʻi during the plantation era, included *ginataang* (dishes cooked in coconut milk). Coconut-based stews, like *ginataang gulay* (vegetables in coconut milk), and desserts like *biko* (a sweet coconut sticky rice cake) became popular among the local community.

Coconut is occasionally used in Japanese-inspired sweets, adding a tropical twist to traditional treats like mochi. While mochi is typically made with glutinous rice flour and filled with red bean paste or other classic ingredients, coconut milk or coconut flakes are sometimes incorporated to create a unique variation. Coconut is also used as a topping for some modern variations of *daifuku* (filled mochi) or as part of mochi-based desserts, blending tropical and Japanese elements. Thai cuisine, which has become increasingly popular in Hawai'i, features coconut milk in soups and curries—the creaminess of coconut milk balances the heat of Thai spices.

Latin American dishes like ceviche have been embraced in Hawai'i, often incorporating tropical flavors like coconut. In ceviche, fresh fish is marinated in citrus juices, and in Hawai'i, coconut milk is sometimes added to give the dish a creamy texture that complements the tartness of the lime. This fusion creates a unique Hawaiian twist on the traditional Latin American dish, blending the freshness of the Islands' seafood with the richness of coconut.

In Hawai'i's modern cuisine, coconut is used in a variety of ways to create innovative fusion dishes. Coconut-based sauces and dressings complement the fresh seafood that Hawai'i is known for. Coconut milk is often used in poke variations, smoothies, and baked goods, while coconut oil has found popularity as a healthy alternative for frying and cooking. Coconut flakes are used to garnish dishes or are incorporated into desserts like macaroons, cookies, and ice cream.

The ongoing use of coconut in Hawai'i's food culture reflects its historical significance and versatility as an ingredient. Whether enjoyed in a traditional dish like haupia, as a modern addition to poke, or as part of the multicultural culinary tapestry of the Islands, the coconut continues to be a symbol of nourishment, adaptability, and the blending of cultures in Hawai'i.

Coconuts, with their strong Polynesian roots and wide appeal, are a testament to Hawai'i's culinary history and a bridge to the broader Pacific and beyond. Through centuries of migration, trade, and fusion, coconuts have remained at the heart of Island cuisine, celebrated for their flavor, functionality, and cultural importance.

PŪPŪ, SOUPS & SIDES

TROPICAL ISLAND POKE

Serves 4 to 6

The coconut milk and mango dramatically put the "tropical" in this Island poke. It's an interesting combination of textures—'ahi and mango cubes—soaked in soy sauce, sesame oil, and coconut milk. It's a real blend of the South Pacific, Eastern Pacific, and Hawai'i.

2 teaspoons sesame oil
3 tablespoons soy sauce
1 teaspoon finely chopped garlic
2 fresh Hawaiian chili peppers, finely chopped
½ cup coconut milk
1 cup cubed mango (½-inch cubes)
¼ cup chopped cilantro
2 tablespoons lemon juice
1 pound fresh 'ahi fillet, cut into ½-inch cubes
Salt, to taste

Combine all ingredients in a bowl, except 'ahi. Mix well. Add 'ahi to mixture and marinate at least 1 hour before serving. Garnish with chopped cilantro.

SIMPLY 'AHI CEVICHE

Serves 4 to 6

Many Polynesian ceviche recipes call for long marination times. This ceviche is served immediately after it is assembled. The fish is only partially "cooked" by the lime juice—the outside is "cooked" and the inside is still raw. This contrast of flavors and textures is reminiscent of seared sashimi.

1 pound sashimi-grade 'ahi, cut into ¾-inch cubes
2 medium-size cucumbers, peeled, seeded, cut into ¼-inch cubes
2 medium-size round onions, peeled, cut into ¼-inch cubes
2 medium-size fresh tomatoes, trimmed, cut into ¼-inch cubes
½ cup chopped green onion
4 tablespoons chopped cilantro, divided use
Pinch of red chili pepper flakes, or to taste
¼ cup lime juice (about 2 limes)
2 cups coconut milk
Salt and pepper, to taste

Put the 'ahi, cucumber, onion, tomato, green onion, and 2 tablespoons of the cilantro into a bowl. (Reserve 2 tablespoons of cilantro for garnish.) Add the chili flakes. Pour the lime juice into the bowl. Gently stir all of the ingredients together. Add the coconut milk and mix again. Adjust the seasoning with salt and pepper.

Put the fish on individual serving plates or on a platter. Garnish with cilantro and lime slices.

COCONUT SHRIMP

Serves 8 to 10

Roman de Peralta, lead singer and songwriter for the local Hawaiian reggae band, Kolohe Kai, shared this recipe on Cooking Hawaiian Style.

1 (10-ounce) box tempura batter mix
2 (6-ounce) packages panko flakes
1 cup coconut flakes
2 pounds large shrimp, cleaned & deveined
1 cup mochiko flour
Oil for deep-frying
Sweet chili sauce (for dipping)

Mix tempura batter mix according to box instructions. In separate bowl, mix panko with coconut flakes.

Take one cleaned and deveined shrimp at a time and dust with mochiko flour. Shake excess flour off, dip into tempura batter and roll into coconut panko mixture. Fry in hot oil until golden brown. Drain on paper towels.

PAPAYA, MINT, AND COCONUT SOUP

Serves 4

Nothing like a cool soup on a hot Hawaiian day. Ripe papayas and coconut milk make this rich and creamy. You can leave out the rum when the kids are eating.

- 2 medium-size ripe papayas, peeled, seeded, and chopped
- 2 cups coconut milk
- 2 tablespoons dark rum (optional)
- 2 tablespoons mint leaves
- 2 teaspoons honey
- 1 teaspoon island seasoning (combination of nutmeg, cinnamon, thyme, and allspice)

GARNISH

Sprigs of mint

Place the papayas, coconut milk, rum, mint leaves, honey, and island seasoning in a food processor. Purée for 20 to 30 seconds or until mixture is smooth. Refrigerate 1 hour before serving. Garnish each serving with a sprig of mint.

COCONUT CREAM OF CELERY SOUP

Serves 8 to 10

The Kīlauea Lodge in Volcano on the Big Island was once a YMCA retreat center. It still features an international fireplace of friendship: a large fireplace decorated with stones and coins from all over the world. Now a country inn, this soup recipes comes from their restaurant.

10 cups chicken broth
3 pounds celery stalks, cubed
2 pounds russet potatoes, peeled, cubed
2 cups milk
½ cup heavy cream
½ cup coconut syrup
1½ teaspoons celery salt
1 teaspoon white pepper
1 cup (2 sticks) unsalted butter

GARNISH

Parsley, finely chopped

Pour the chicken broth into a large (at least 4 quart) pot and bring it to a boil over medium-high heat. Purée the chopped celery and potatoes in food processor until very fine. Add the purée to the boiling chicken broth and beat with a whip for 2 minutes. Add the milk and heavy cream, then the coconut syrup, and stir to mix. Bring the soup to a boil, then reduce the heat to low. Add the celery salt and white pepper; stir. Cover the pot and let the soup simmer for 40 minutes. Stir frequently.

Remove the pot from the stove. Ladle the soup, bit by bit, into a fine sieve set over a 4-quart bowl. Push the soup through the sieve. After all the soup has been sieved, discard the residue left in the sieve.

Cut the butter into ½-inch pieces and add it to the hot cream of celery soup. Whisk the soup until the butter has dissolved.

Ladle the soup into soup bowls and sprinkle with chopped parsley.

HILO HULI MUSHROOM SOUP

Serves 8 to 10

Hilo Huli is an annual fundraiser for the Rotary Club of South Hilo. It is held on the first Sunday in May at Coconut Island or Mokuola Island. Chef Albert Jeyte of Kīlauea Lodge created this wonderful soup for the 5th annual Hilo Huli.

1 cup diced red bell pepper (⅛-inch dice)
1 cup diced green bell pepper (⅛-inch dice)
1 cup diced round onions (⅛-inch dice)
½ pound diced button or white mushrooms (⅛-inch dice)
¾ cup finely-chopped garlic
¼ cup (½ stick) butter
1 teaspoon dried oregano
1 teaspoon dried marjoram
1 teaspoon finely ground black pepper
1 teaspoon salt
1 cup flour
12 cups chicken broth
¼ cup plus 2 tablespoons sweet curry powder
12 ounces sour cream
1 (13.5 ounce) can coconut milk

GARNISH
4 tablespoons butter
¾ ounces sweetened coconut flakes

CORNSTARCH SLURRY
½ cup cold water
2 tablespoons cornstarch

Dice the bell peppers, onion, mushrooms, and chop garlic per the instructions in the ingredients list.

Put the butter in a large 1-gallon stockpot over low heat. When the butter is melted, add the peppers, onions, mushrooms, garlic, oregano, marjoram, black pepper, and salt. Sauté for 6 to 7 minutes , stirring occasionally, until the peppers and onions have softened.

Add the flour and stir for 4 to 5 minutes. The flour and melted butter will combine to make a golden roux, the flour-butter paste that is the basis of many sauces. Slowly add the chicken broth, whisking constantly. The stock should thicken. The whisking prevents lumps. Turn the heat up to high and bring the sauce to a boil, continuing to whisk constantly. Turn down the heat again, whisk in the curry powder, and simmer the mixture, covered, for about 20 minutes. Occasionally remove the lid and stir.

While the soup is simmering, prepare the coconut for the garnish. Melt the butter in a sauté pan over low heat. Add the coconut flakes and cook, stirring constantly, until the coconut flakes are light to dark brown.

When you are ready to serve the soup, add the sour cream and coconut milk and bring to a slow boil again. Turn down the heat and simmer an additional 5 minutes, until sour cream is incorporated into the soup. Mix the cornstarch and water to form a slurry and add to the soup, stirring constantly as the soup thickens.

Pour the soup into soup bowls and sprinkle with toasted coconut flakes.

CHEF LEE ANNE WONG'S DUMPLINGS WITH LEMON-GRASS BROTH

Serves 4 to 6

This dumpling recipe also appears in Lee Anne's cookbook, Dumplings All Day Wong, *which is a must-have for those of you who love dumplings!*

DUMPLINGS

¾ pound ground white chicken meat
2 tablespoons finely minced lemongrass
2 tablespoons finely minced shallots
3 cloves garlic, finely minced
2 tablespoons seeded and minced jalapeño pepper
1 teaspoon ground turmeric
1 tablespoon brown sugar
1 tablespoon cornstarch
1 tablespoon fish sauce
¼ cup full-fat coconut milk
Zest of ½ lime
1 tablespoon lime juice
½ teaspoon salt
30 round dumpling wrappers

LEMONGRASS BROTH
8 cups chicken stock
½ cup sliced yellow onion
1 stalk lemongrass, crushed and chopped
3 cloves garlic, crushed
1 (2-inch) piece of ginger, sliced
1 piece lime zest ½-inch × 2-inch
1 tablespoon lime juice
Salt and sugar, to taste
1 cup thinly sliced scallion greens soaked in iced water
1 cup cilantro leaves and stems

GARNISH
1 teaspoon fried shallots (per bowl)

In a large bowl, combine ground chicken, lemongrass, shallots, garlic, and jalapeño pepper. In a small bowl, mix the turmeric, sugar, and cornstarch, then sprinkle evenly over the filling. Add the fish sauce, coconut milk, lime zest, lime juice, and salt to the bowl and mix the filling well. Refrigerate until needed.

Fill each wrapper with 1 tablespoon of filling. Lightly wet the edges of the wrapper and form the dumpling using the classic pleat technique. Keep the dumplings covered on a lightly floured tray or plate.

To make the broth, in a pot, bring chicken stock, onion, lemongrass, garlic, ginger, and lime zest to a boil over high heat. Reduce the heat to a rolling simmer and cook for 30 minutes. Strain the broth through a fine-mesh sieve and season to taste with the lime juice, salt, and sugar. Keep warm.

Bring a large pot of water to a boil over high heat. Add half the dumplings to the pot. When the water boils again, add ½ cup of cold water. When the water boils again, add another ½ cup of cold water. When the water boils again (the dumplings should be floating), drain the dumplings and add to the chicken broth. Cook the remaining dumplings and add to the broth. Add the scallion and cilantro and serve soup hot, garnished with fried shallots.

TAHITIAN CRABMEAT SOUP

Serves 8

In Hawai'i, crabs come in many shapes, colors, and sizes, depending on where they live. Live crabs should be covered in a brine solution (⅓ cup salt, one gallon of water) for thirty minutes so that they can naturally filter themselves clean. Prepare as quickly as possible so they're fresh when they arrive on the dining room table.

- 2 cups diced onion
- ¼ cup butter
- 2 tablespoons flour
- 2 cups heavy cream
- 1½ cups chicken stock
- 2 cups coconut milk
- 2 cups chopped frozen spinach (thawed) or 3 cups chopped fresh spinach, washed and stemmed
- 1½ cups crabmeat
- Salt and white pepper, to taste

In a large saucepan sauté onion in butter until translucent. Stir in flour; blend well. Add heavy cream and chicken stock; simmer for 5 minutes, stirring frequently. Stir in coconut milk, spinach, and crabmeat. Cook for 3 minutes, stirring frequently. Season to taste with salt and white pepper.

COCONUT THAI RICE

Serves 4

- 1 cup jasmine or other long grain rice
- 2 teaspoons canola oil
- 1 cup chopped onion
- 1 teaspoon peeled and minced ginger
- 3 garlic cloves, peeled and minced
- 1 cup crushed pineapple with liquid
- ¾ cup water
- 1 (15-ounce) can coconut milk
- ½ teaspoon kosher salt

Rinse jasmine or long grain rice under cold running water until water runs clear. Let drain. Set aside.

In a large saucepan, heat oil over medium heat and sauté onion and ginger until onion is translucent. Add garlic and stir for about 30 seconds. Stir in rice, pineapple, and water and cover. Reduce heat to low and simmer until rice is tender and liquid is absorbed (about 20 minutes). Remove from heat and stir in coconut milk. Let stand, covered, for 5 minutes.

Sprinkle salt over rice and distribute by tossing with a fork.

BAKED SWEET POTATOES

Serves 6 to 12

This dish is good any time of year. Butter the pan, dot the sweet potatoes with more butter. Add raisins, more butter, macadamia nuts, and more butter. Drizzle with coconut syrup and add just a bit more butter!

6 pounds sweet potatoes, cooked and thinly sliced
1 pound butter, divided use
½ cup packed brown sugar
1 cup raisins
Salt and pepper, to taste
½ cup all-purpose flour
½ cup chopped macadamia nuts
4 ounces coconut syrup

Preheat oven to 350°F. Rub a casserole dish with butter and spread the sweet potato slices on bottom. Dot with butter, brown sugar, raisins, salt, and pepper. Bake for 40 minutes. When done, combine the flour, macadamia nuts, remaining butter and coconut syrup until it is dry and resembles crumbly pie dough. Top the casserole with the macadamia mixture and bake until it is golden brown, 30 to 40 minutes.

BAKED COCONUT TARO

Serves 4

Taro has been a staple in Hawai'i from earliest times to the present. The entire plant is eaten, from its starchy root (often mashed into poi) to its heart-shaped leaves (known as lū'au). Over 300 varieties of taro are cultivated world-wide; eighty-six of those varieties are grown in Hawai'i. Wetland taro is grown in flooded valley fields and is best for poi. Dryland taro tolerates dryer conditions and can be cultivated in the uplands. In this recipe, the sweetness of the coconut syrup mix enhances the flavor of the taro.

1 pound fresh taro root, blanched and cubed
¼ cup butter
¼ cup coconut syrup
Salt and pepper, to taste

GARNISH

¼ cup coconut flakes, toasted in skillet or under broiler
Macadamia nuts, roasted and chopped

Preheat oven to 350°F. Combine all ingredients in a covered casserole dish and bake for 35 minutes. To serve, garnish with coconut flakes and macadamia nuts.

SWEET POTATO COCONUT CASSEROLE

Serves 6

If you want to start a new holiday tradition, serve this fresh coconut and macadamia nut version of the classic sweet potato dish. Your family may never want that old marshmallow topped version again.

4 cups sweet potatoes steamed until soft and mashed
⅓ cup butter
½ cup milk
½ cup coconut milk
⅓ cup grated fresh coconut
⅓ cup toasted and chopped macadamia nuts
⅓ cup brown sugar
2 tablespoons butter, melted

Preheat oven to 325°F. Whisk potatoes, butter, milk, and coconut milk until light and fluffy. Prepare 2-quart casserole with vegetable oil spray. Pour potato mixture into casserole. Mix coconut, macadamia nuts, brown sugar, and melted butter. Sprinkle coconut mixture on top of the sweet potatoes. Bake for 1 hour or until potatoes are heated through the top is crunchy.

MAIN DISHES

CHICKEN AFRITADA

Serves 4 to 5

Afritada is a traditional recipe using chicken, pork, or liver, with potatoes, carrots, and tomato sauce. This recipe includes a twist: coconut milk for richness.

¼ cup canola oil
2 pounds boneless chicken thighs, cut into 1½-inch pieces
4 cloves garlic, minced
1 medium onion, diced
1 red bell pepper, small dice
1 (8-ounce) can tomato sauce
2 cups coconut milk
1½ cups chicken broth
2 bay leaves
1 large potato, quartered
1 large carrot, sliced
2 cups bias-cut green beans
Salt and ground black pepper, to taste

GARNISH

1 tablespoon sliced green onion

Heat oil in large pot. Sauté chicken until golden brown on each side. Remove and set aside. In same pot, sauté garlic, onions, and bell pepper until onions are tender. Return chicken to pot along with any drippings. Add tomato sauce, coconut milk, chicken broth, and bay leaves; simmer 25 to 30 minutes or until chicken is tender. Add potato and carrots; simmer another 10 minutes. Once vegetables are tender, add green beans; taste and adjust seasonings with salt and pepper. Serve with fresh, sliced green onions.

Tip: The bell pepper can be puréed instead of diced, which spreads the flavor through every bite.

CHICKEN SATAY WITH PEANUT SAUCE

Makes 32 skewers

This recipe comes from Sous-chef Bryceson Velez of the Mauna Lani Bay Hotel and Bungalows. Although it seems long and complicated, the only part of it that requires much work is the optional lemongrass in the peanut sauce. You may want to double the amount of sauce; it's good with so many foods: noodles, steamed vegetables, grilled meat, and poultry.

2 pounds boneless, skinless chicken thighs
32 bamboo skewers

SATAY MARINADE

1½ tablespoons chopped garlic
1½ teaspoons ground coriander
1½ teaspoons ground cumin
1½ tablespoons curry powder
¼ teaspoon turmeric
¼ cup sugar
1½ tablespoons grated ginger
1½ tablespoons fish sauce or Thai nam pla
1 cup coconut milk
1½ tablespoons water
¼ teaspoon kosher salt

To marinate the chicken, cut each thigh (you'll have about 8) into 4 even pieces. Chop the garlic and mix all marinade ingredients thoroughly. Reserve 2 tablespoons of marinade before dipping chicken; set aside. Place chicken pieces on skewers and dip in the marinade. Cover and leave in the refrigerator for 3 hours. Turn the chicken pieces occasionally so that they marinate evenly.

Grill chicken skewers over hot coals or an electric grill, 5 minutes on each side, until chicken is thoroughly cooked. Serve with Peanut Sauce on the side.

PEANUT SAUCE

- 1 stalk lemongrass (optional)
- 1 kaffir lime leaf, bruised but left whole
- 1 to 2 teaspoons red Thai curry paste, or to taste
- Canola oil for sautéing
- 1 cup coconut milk
- ½ cup peanut butter (more if you want it thicker)
- 2 tablespoons chicken marinade

GARNISH

- 2 tablespoons chopped roasted peanuts

If you are using lemongrass in the peanut sauce: strip off any dried leaves and cut off the bulb. Cut across the stem at ¼-inch intervals, or closer, until you have a stack of tiny rounds. Put the rounds into a food processor and process until you have a pile of lemongrass fragments. These should soften when cooked in the sauce. You may want to taste the finished sauce to check; if the lemongrass bits are still dry and hard, you may need to strain them out. The upper half of the stalk will probably be too dry to cook this way. You can use it in the sauce if you make a series of shallow cuts crosswise on the stalk and bend it a few times, to bruise it and release the juices. Let it simmer in the sauce and them remove it before serving.

To prepare the peanut sauce, crush the lime leaves. Fry the leaves and the Thai curry paste in a little canola oil until they start to smell spicy and delicious. This should take only 30 seconds or so. Add the remaining ingredients and simmer for 5 minutes. Turn off heat and let the sauce steep for another 15 minutes before cooling. Remove the lime leaves and any lemongrass stalks before serving. Garnish sauce with chopped peanuts.

MAILE SYMMOND'S EVIL PRINCESS

Serves 2

2 tablespoons cooking oil
½ cup sliced round onion
1 teaspoon peeled and minced garlic
1 cup chopped skinless and boned chicken breast
½ cup chopped long beans (1-inch pieces)
½ cup thinly sliced bamboo shoots
¼ cup chicken stock
2 tablespoons red curry paste
1 tablespoon oyster sauce
1 teaspoon fish sauce
⅓ tablespoon sugar
½ cup coconut milk
Cornstarch mixture (2 tablespoons water + 1 tablespoon cornstarch)
1 cup Thai basil

Heat up wok, make sure your wok is smoking hot, then add oil. Toss in onions, fry for 30 seconds, then add minced garlic (be careful not to burn the garlic). In order, add chicken breast, long beans, bamboo shoots, and chicken stock; toss for a minute. Then add red curry paste, oyster sauce, fish sauce, and sugar. Mix with spatula. Add coconut milk and a little bit of cornstarch to thicken. Simmer until bubbling, then at the last moment toss in Thai basil and plate.

CHICKEN PANANG WITH MACADAMIA NUTS

Serves 4

The use of macadamia nuts in Chef Gordon Lum's panang takes this recipe over the top!

2 pounds chicken thighs, deboned
Salt and pepper
1 cup flour (for dredging)
1 sliced bell pepper (any color)
1 sliced onion
3 finely diced kaffir lime leaves
3 tablespoons roughly ground Island Princess Hawai'i macadamia nuts
¼ cup oil
2½ tablespoons panang curry paste
1 (19-ounce) can coconut milk
2 tablespoons turbinado or raw sugar
2 teaspoons fish sauce, to taste
4 to 5 Thai basil leaves (optional)

Rinse, then dry, the boned chicken thighs. Lightly salt and pepper the thighs on both sides and then dredge in flour, shaking off the excess flour.

Heat a Dutch oven and add enough oil to quickly brown chicken. Sear both sides of thighs until it becomes a light golden brown (about ¾ cooked). Set thighs aside.

While they are cooling, slice the bell pepper and onion. Finely dice the kaffir lime leaves and roughly grind or chop the macadamia nuts.

After the chicken thighs cool, cut into chunks. Heat the oil and add the curry paste, searing the paste for a minute. Add the chicken chunks and stir until the chunks are coated with the paste. Add the peppers and onion and stir until they are also coated. Add the coconut milk, kaffir lime leaves, turbinado sugar, macadamia nuts, and fish sauce to the pot. Bring to a boil, then lower the heat and simmer for about 10 to 15 minutes. Garnish with basil leaves.

CHEF IPPY AIONA'S PORK BELLY ADOBO

Serves 4

MARINADE

1 orange, sliced
1 lemon, sliced
2 cups apple cider vinegar or sugar cane vinegar
2 garlic cloves, crushed
2 bay leaves, crushed
1 cup water

2 pounds pork belly
3 to 4 tablespoons cooking oil
2 cloves garlic, crushed
6 to 8 peppercorns
2 bay leaves, crushed
1 tablespoon Dijon mustard
½ cup soy sauce
2 cans coconut milk
2 cups brown sugar

Mix marinade ingredients in a large glass bowl or Ziploc bag. Place pork belly in marinade and soak overnight, if possible.

Take pork out of marinade and slice into 2-inch cubes. Reserve marinade.

Brown pork on medium-high heat in oil with garlic, peppercorns, bay leaves, and Dijon mustard. Once browned, add enough of the marinade used earlier to barely cover meat. Add soy sauce, coconut milk, and sugar. Cook on medium/low heat until tender about 1 to 2 hours.

BICOL EXPRESS–SPICY PORK BELLY IN COCONUT MILK

Serves 4 to 5

Bicol Express is a dish that will make you sweat. Fiery with chilies, it is not for the heat-averse. Coconut milk and shrimp paste provide sweet-salty balance and richness. The dish is said to be named for the train that runs from Manila to the Bicol region. Enjoy it over some jasmine rice.

3 tablespoons vegetable oil
2 tablespoons minced garlic
1 cup minced onion
3 tablespoons minced ginger
2 pounds pork belly, sliced into strips
¼ cup dried shrimp paste
3 cups coconut milk
3 to 4 adobong sili or serrano peppers, cut on bias
Salt and pepper, to taste

Heat oil in skillet. Add garlic and sauté 2 minutes or until garlic is cooked (be careful garlic does not burn). Add onions and ginger, then pork; cook 8 to 10 minutes or until pork starts to brown. Stir in dried shrimp paste.

Add coconut milk and peppers; simmer 20 to 30 minutes or until pork is tender. Season with salt and pepper to taste.

Tip: Taste your chilies for the heat factor before adding them to any dish. You don't want to ruin your dish, and there's no going back.

SOUTH PACIFIC COCONUT RICE WITH SAUTÉED PORK LOIN

Serves 4

The coconut rice is topped with what is probably one of the best pestos ever. Then, the tender pork loin is laid on top and covered in fried onions.

4 cups Basmati rice
2 cups coconut milk
2 cups chicken stock or low-sodium chicken broth
4 tablespoons Ginger Pesto
¼ cup light vegetable oil
1 cup diced onions
1 cup all-purpose flour
Pinch of salt and pepper
1 tablespoon oil
6 (2½-ounce) pieces pork loin

GARNISH

½ cup thinly sliced fried onions

Cook rice with coconut milk and stock. Cook as if using only water. When rice is cooked, dollop a little ginger pesto on top.

Meanwhile, heat ¼ cup salad oil in a wok. Dust onions with flour, salt, and pepper. Shake off all excess flour and fry in oil until golden brown. Remove and place on paper towel to drain.

In a separate wok, heat 1 tablespoon of oil. Dust pork with flour, salt, and pepper. Cook in hot oil about 2 minutes on each side.

Serve with pork on top of rice with pesto; top with onions.

GINGER PESTO

Makes about 2 cups

- 1 teaspoon salt
- ½ cup peeled and minced fresh ginger
- ½ cup minced green onions
- ½ cup lightly packed minced fresh cilantro
- ¼ teaspoon white pepper
- 1 cup salad oil

In a large mixing bowl, combine all ingredients for the pesto except for the salad oil. Mix thoroughly with a wire whisk. Gradually add salad oil while continually whisking until all oil is incorporated.

KĀLUA LŪ‘AU LASAGNA ROLLS WITH HAUPIA BÉCHAMEL SAUCE

Serves 4

2 packages frozen taro leaves (lū‘au) or spinach
8 lasagna noodles, prepared according to directions
6 tablespoons butter (use margarine or oil for vegetarian)
6 tablespoons flour
2 (12-ounce) cans of coconut milk
Salt and pepper, to taste
1 container kālua pork or 1 pound homemade kālua pork
¼ cup milk

Empty lū‘au leaves into a sieve and squeeze out all of the excess liquid. Set aside. Prepare lasagna noodles. Once cooked, set aside.

Melt butter or margarine in sauce pan. Once butter is melted add flour slowly, whisking constantly. Cook flour for about 1 minute. Slowly add coconut milk whisking constantly to maintain a smooth consistency. Salt and pepper to taste. Set béchamel aside.

Preheat oven to 325°F. Divide lūʻau leaves into 8 equal portions. Take a piece of lasagna noodle and spread the lūʻau leaf across ¾ of the length of the pasta. Take kālua pork and spread across ¾ of the length of the pasta. Spread about 2 tablespoons of the béchamel over the taro leaves and kālua pork and roll. Carefully place rolled lasagna into a shallow 8 x 8-inch glass or ceramic baking pan. Continue until all 8 rolls are complete. Take remaining béchamel and thin it out with milk; pour over lasagna rolls. Bake covered for 20 to 25 minutes.

COCONUT-CURRY HALEAKALĀ RANCH LAMB CHOPS WITH MANGO SALSA

Serves 4

Maui Cattle Company's Haleakalā Ranch lamb comes from herds raised on the slopes of the majestic volcano. These free-range, grass-fed animals can be seen grazing as you drive the Upcountry roads. The meat is tender and flavorful. It's sold in a few Upcountry and Kula markets.

2 racks of lamb, cut into double-bone chops

MARINADE

½ cup soy sauce
1 cup coconut cream (top 8-ounce portion of the can of coconut milk)
3 tablespoons curry powder
2 tablespoons minced garlic
1 tablespoon brown cane sugar

SALSA

2 cups diced mango
¼ cup diced red onion (¼-inch dice)

¼ cup diced bell pepper (¼-inch dice)
4 sprigs mint leaves (discard stems), chopped
2 tablespoons fresh lime juice (1 average lime)
¼ cup olive oil
Salt and pepper, to taste

Mix all the marinade ingredients in a bowl. Place the lamb chops in the marinade. Coat well, cover, and refrigerate for 4 hours. Turn after two hours so the lamb can marinate evenly.

Make the fresh salsa while the lamb is marinating. Prepare the mango, red onion, bell pepper, mint, and lime juice according to the ingredient list. Mix all ingredients in a small bowl, cover, and set aside.

Grill the marinated lamb over medium heat. If you are using kiawe charcoal, make sure the coals are covered with a coating of light ash once the fire has died down. This will allow the lamb to cook without burning and will give the lamb a nice smoky taste when grilled.

Remove the lamb chops from the grill, plate, and serve topped with the fresh mango salsa.

GINGER PESTO-CRUSTED 'ŌPAKAPAKA WITH COCONUT CREAM SAUCE

Serves 4

GINGER PESTO SAUCE

½ cup minced fresh cilantro
½ cup minced green onion
¼ cup minced fresh ginger
¾ cup peanut oil
1 tablespoon soy sauce
Salt and white pepper, to taste

COCONUT CREAM SAUCE

3 tablespoons butter
1 medium round onion, minced
1 cup heavy cream
2 cups canned coconut milk (unsweetened)
2 tablespoons cornstarch mixed with 1½ tablespoons water, if needed for thickening
Salt and pepper, to taste

8 (3-ounce) fresh 'ōpakapaka (pink snapper) fillets
1 tablespoon oil, for frying

GARNISH

Tomato wedges
Enoki (straw) mushrooms

To prepare the Ginger Pesto Sauce, place cilantro, green onions, and ginger in a deep bowl. Heat peanut oil in a pan until smoking. Pour heated oil over cilantro, green onions, and ginger. BE CAREFUL: The OIL WILL BE SIZZLING AND VERY HOT. Add soy sauce and salt and pepper to taste. Set aside.

To prepare the Coconut Cream Sauce, place butter in a saucepan. Add onions and cook until translucent. Add heavy cream. Bring to a boil, reduce heat, and simmer for 1 to 2 minutes. Add coconut milk and cook for another 2 minutes. Set aside. If the Coconut Cream Sauce isn't thick enough, don't panic. Just add enough cornstarch mixture to thicken the simmering sauce as desired, and cook for another minute. Adjust the seasoning with salt and pepper.

To prepare the ʻōpakapaka, marinate fillets in cooled Ginger Pesto Sauce for 1 to 2 minutes. Place fillets in a frying pan, and cook for 1½ to 2 minutes on each side over medium-high heat.

Pour 2 ounces of Coconut Cream Sauce on each of 4 serving plates. Arrange two pieces of fish on each plate, and drizzle with Ginger Pesto Sauce.

SEARED ALBACORE TUNA WITH COCONUT-GINGER SAUCE

Serves 4

- 4 (6-ounce, ¾-inch thick) albacore tuna steaks
- 2 tablespoons oil
- Seafood Marinade (see p. 59)
- Coconut-Ginger Sauce (see p. 59)

Marinate tuna steaks in Seafood Marinade for 10 minutes.

Heat oil in a frying pan over high heat. Sear marinated tuna for 2 minutes on each side. Serve hot with warm Coconut-Ginger Sauce.

SEAFOOD MARINADE

1 cup soy sauce
1 tablespoon oyster sauce
1 tablespoon sesame oil
½ cup brown sugar
1 tablespoon chopped cilantro
1 teaspoon chili flakes
1 teaspoon minced garlic
¼ teaspoon Chinese five-spice powder

Mix all ingredients until sugar is dissolved.

COCONUT-GINGER SAUCE

1 can coconut milk
¼ cup sugar
1 tablespoon minced ginger
1½ tablespoons cornstarch mixed with 3 tablespoons water for thickening
Salt and pepper, to taste

In a saucepan, combine coconut milk, sugar, and ginger. Bring to a boil. Mix cornstarch and water together and whisk into coconut milk and ginger sauce to thicken. Season with salt and pepper.

CURRIED MAHIMAHI

Serves 2 to 4

4 mahimahi fillets
1 egg, beaten
Flour for dredging
2 to 3 tablespoons butter

CURRY SAUCE

1 small onion, sliced
2 tablespoons butter
2 tablespoons flour
2 to 3 tablespoons curry powder
3 tablespoons applesauce
¾ cup chicken stock
¾ cup coconut milk
1 jigger Marsala wine or cream sherry

GARNISH

Chopped chives or parsley
Slivered toasted almonds

Preheat oven to 325°F. Dip fish fillets in beaten egg and then in flour. Brown in butter and place in shallow casserole dish; set aside.

To prepare Curry Sauce, cook onion in butter until soft. Do not brown. Remove from stove. Add flour, curry powder, and applesauce. Cook over low heat and stir in chicken stock. Add coconut milk and wine or sherry.

Pour sauce over mahimahi and bake for 20 minutes. Garnish with chives or parsley and almonds.

SQUID LŪ'AU

Serves 4

4 cups cooked lū'au leaves (start with 5 pounds of raw leaves)

2 cups chopped squid, cleaned (start with 2 pounds of squid)
¼ cup butter
2 cups coconut milk
Hawaiian salt, to taste

To prepare the lū'au leaves, cut off about ½-inch from each of the three points of the leaf tips. Cut off the stem, right next to the leaf. Peel off the large vein that runs along the center of the leaf. Put the leaves in a large pot, add water to cover and a pinch of baking soda (about 1 teaspoon), and bring to a boil. Cook for about 15 minutes. Drain. Put the leaves in the pot again, add water and baking soda again, and boil for another 15 minutes. Drain and boil for one last time. You'll probably need to cook the leaves for 45 minutes total (15 + 15 + 15). Taste the leaves at the end; if they aren't tender, cook them a little longer.

Cut the cleaned squid into ½-inch pieces.

Melt the butter in a large pot over medium heat. Stir in the cooked lūʻau leaves and cook until warm and soft. Add the coconut milk and mix well. Stir in the squid and add salt to taste. Add more coconut milk if you feel the mixture is too thick. Increase the heat slightly, bring to a boil, and immediately turn off the heat. Serve immediately.

Note: Add the squid only at the end and cook it briefly. This is one way to make sure that it's tender and tasty.

COCONUT MAC NUT SHRIMP WITH GUAVA SWEET & SOUR SAUCE

Serves 4

This dish blends a variety of textures, flavors, and aromas. Adding the coconut flakes makes all the difference. The shrimps will crisp up into spiny-looking prongs that crackle when you bite into them. Panko is a Japanese-style breadcrumb mixture that gives an extra crunchy texture to foods.

1 cup coconut flakes
1 cup crushed roasted macadamia nuts
2½ cups panko (Japanese-style crispy breadcrumbs)
24 pieces shrimp (21/25 count), cleaned and shelled
1 cup all-purpose flour
3 or 4 whole eggs, whipped
Salt and pepper, to taste
4 cups vegetable oil

To prepare shrimp, mix coconut flakes, macadamia nuts, and panko together. Dredge the shrimp in flour, egg, and then in coconut flake-macadamia nut-panko mixture. Season with salt and pepper. Deep-fry until golden brown. Serve with Sam Choy's Guava Sweet & Sour Sauce.

SAM CHOY'S GUAVA SWEET & SOUR SAUCE

- ½ cup ketchup
- ½ cup white wine vinegar
- ½ cup water
- 2 teaspoons soy sauce
- ½ cup granulated sugar
- ¼ cup frozen guava concentrate, undiluted
- 1½ teaspoons minced fresh garlic
- ¼ teaspoon hot pepper sauce
- ¼ cup pineapple juice
- 4 tablespoons cornstarch mixed with 3 tablespoons water, for thickening

In a medium saucepan, combine all sweet and sour ingredients except cornstarch mixture. Blend well, bring to a boil, then add cornstarch mixture. Reduce heat and simmer, stirring frequently until thickened.

HAWAIIAN SHRIMP CURRY

Serves 6

¼ cup butter or margarine
1 small onion, minced
1 clove garlic, minced
1 small piece ginger root, minced
1½ tablespoons curry powder
⅓ cup flour
1½ teaspoons salt
1 (12-ounce) can coconut milk
1¼ cups chicken broth
1¾ pounds medium shrimp, shelled and cleaned

CONDIMENTS
Chutney
Minced green onion
Chopped hard-boiled eggs
Chopped macadamia nuts
Shredded coconut
Chopped raisins
Crisp crumbled bacon

Melt butter or margarine in saucepan and sauté onion, garlic, and ginger until tender. Add curry powder, flour, and salt. Slowly stir in coconut milk and broth. Cover over medium heat, stirring constantly, until mixture thickens.

Stir in shrimp. Cook until shrimp turns pink and heated through. Serve over hot steamed rice with condiments of choice.

MELVEEN LEED'S CRUSTACEAN POLYNESIA

Serves 4

Local singer Melveen Leed shares this delicious Tahitian-influenced dish.

- 4 to 5 cups fresh or canned coconut milk
- 1 tomato
- 1 Maui onion, diced small
- 4 to 5 pounds of your favorite seafood: whole crab, cut up; lobster tail, cut in half; clams; shrimp (shell on)
- Salt and pepper, to taste

In a large pot, put coconut milk, tomato, and onion and stir. Then immediately add crustaceans and stir all ingredients together. Cover pot and cook on medium-high heat until it starts to boil, then reduce to simmer. Dish is ready when you see the crab, shrimp, and lobster turn red. Salt and pepper, to taste.

ARROZ VALENCIANA (PAELLA)

Serves 4 to 5

This is a one-pot mauka-meets-makai dish that includes chicken, sausage, and seafood. It may seem like a lot of ingredients, but it comes together quickly. Think of it as a cross between Arroz Caldo (Filipino congee) and the Cajun classic of Dirty Rice, Filipino-style.

1 cup uncooked Thai jasmine or long-grain rice
½ cup uncooked short-grain rice
Water
2 tablespoons olive oil
3 cloves garlic, crushed
1 onion, cut into chunks
4 boneless chicken thighs, cut into quarters
1 Portuguese sausage, sliced
2 tablespoons tomato purée
1 tablespoon patis (fish sauce)
1 teaspoon safflower, toasted and crushed
2 potatoes, cut into big chunks
1 cup chicken stock
1 cup coconut milk
½ sweet red pepper, cut into chunks
⅓ cup raisins
2 cups chopped raw shrimp
⅓ cup frozen green peas

Soak the rice in water to cover for an hour. Drain well. Set aside.

Preheat oven to 300°F. Heat a sauté pan and add olive oil. Sauté garlic until light brown, then add onions; cook until onions are translucent. Add chicken and sausage; stir and cook 10 minutes. Add rice, tomato purée and patis; stir well and cook 3 to 5 minutes. Add safflower, potatoes, chicken stock, and coconut milk; bring to boil. Reduce heat to low and simmer, covered, for 5 minutes. Stir in sweet peppers and raisins.

Transfer to oven-proof dish. Set this dish into a larger pan and add water to reach halfway up the sides of the dish. Cover both pans tightly with foil. Bake 30 minutes, remove from oven, stir and bake another 30 minutes. Remove from oven, add shrimp and peas; cover and let sit 10 to 12 minutes, allowing the heat of the rice to finish the cooking.

CURRIED LOBSTER WITH FRIED HAUPIA

Serves 4

⅓ cup diced carrots
3 tablespoons frozen peas
½ potato, cut into 1-inch cubes and soaked in water
½ cup chicken broth
¼ cup coconut milk
2 tablespoons half-and-half cream
2 to 3 tablespoons curry powder
⅛ teaspoon salt
⅛ teaspoon pepper
2 tablespoons oil
3 tablespoons diced onion
1 (8-ounce) lobster tail, remove shell and cut into 1½-inch cubes
2 tablespoons cornstarch mixed with 2 tablespoons chicken broth
2 to 3 tablespoons raisins
8 deep-fried haupia pieces

Boil carrots until just done. Add peas just to blanch. Drain and set aside.

Drain potato and pat dry with paper towel. Deep-fry potato for 2 minutes on medium heat or until cooked. Set aside.

In a small bowl, combine chicken broth, coconut milk, half-and-half cream, curry powder, salt and pepper; mix together. Set aside.

Heat a wok or pan on high heat, add oil, then reduce heat slightly. Stir-fry onion and lobster for 2 minutes or until cooked thoroughly. Add chicken broth mixture. Stir-fry for 1 minute more. Stir cornstarch mixture into the work. Add potatoes, carrots, peas, and raisins. Bring to a boil. (Add more chicken broth, if desired, so gravy is of desired consistency.)

Transfer to a serving dish and garnish with deep-fried haupia on the side.

DEEP-FRIED HAUPIA

Serves 4

1½ cups coconut milk
¾ cup water
⅓ cup sugar
5 tablespoons cornstarch

EGG WASH
1 egg
1 cup water
1 tablespoon flour

- 3 tablespoons cornstarch for dusting
- Oil for deep-frying

In a double boiler, heat coconut milk. In a separate bowl, stir together water, sugar, and 5 tablespoons cornstarch until smooth. Stir into coconut milk and cook over low heat until thickened, stirring constantly. Increase temperature slightly and stir vigorously to prevent burning. Mixture should be thick. Pour mixture into an 8-inch square pan. Refrigerate to set.

Cut haupia into 24 pieces, each 2 x 1½ inches. Dip in egg wash, dust with cornstarch, and deep-fry for 2 minutes.

Place haupia around curried lobster. Since only 8 fried haupia is needed, you can choose to fry the rest or keep the remainder as is.

DESSERTS

COCONUT-PINEAPPLE CREAM CAKE

Serves 18 to 24

CAKE

1 box Duncan Hines Lemon Supreme cake mix
4 eggs
½ cup oil
1 cup 7-Up

CREAM CHEESE TOPPING

1 (8-ounce) package cream cheese
1 (12-ounce) can frozen coconut milk, thawed
1 (3-ounce) box instant vanilla pudding

PINEAPPLE COCONUT TOPPING

1 (16-ounce) can crushed pineapple, drained
1 (8-ounce) container Cool Whip
1 can fresh frozen coconut or 1⅓ cups shredded coconut

To make the cake, preheat oven to 350°F. Combine all cake ingredients and beat 3 minutes. Bake in a well-greased and floured 9 x 13-inch pan for 30 to 35 minutes. Cool.

To make the Cream Cheese Topping, whip together all ingredients and spread over cooled cake.

To make the Pineapple Coconut Topping, spread pineapple over cream-cheese topping. Then spread Cool Whip over pineapple. Sprinkle coconut on top. Refrigerate.

PIÑA COLADA POUND CAKE

Serves 12 to 15

If you like piña coladas…here's a pound cake that tastes like the ultimate lounge lizard drink, with coconut and a splash of pineapple.

1½ cups all-purpose flour
1½ cups cake flour
¼ teaspoon salt
1 cup butter, softened
2½ cups sugar
4 eggs, room temperature
½ teaspoon pure lemon extract
½ teaspoon vanilla extract
6 ounces sour cream
3 tablespoons unsweetened coconut milk
¾ cup shredded coconut

PINEAPPLE GLAZE

2 tablespoons unsalted butter, melted
1½ to 2 cups powdered sugar
¼ cup pineapple juice from the can
1teaspoon vanilla extract

Grease and flour two loaf pans. Preheat oven to 350°F. Sift flours and salt; set aside. Beat butter and sugar until light and creamy. Add eggs one at a time. Add lemon and vanilla extracts; mix well. Alternately mix in dry ingredients and sour cream, starting with dry and ending with dry ingredients. Reduce speed and slowly incorporate coconut milk and coconut flakes. Divide batter evenly in loaf pans. Bake for 1¼ hours. To test doneness, insert toothpick to the middle of cake. If it comes out clean, it's done. Transfer to wire rack and cool cake in pan for 30 minutes. Invert warm cakes on parchment paper over rack.

While the cake bakes, make the pineapple glaze. Whisk the melted butter with powdered sugar, pineapple juice, and vanilla extract until well-combined. Add more juice for a thinner glaze or more sugar for a thicker glaze.

YUMMY COCONUT APPLE CAKE

Serves 18 to 24

1 cup butter or margarine
5 to 7 fresh baking apples, cored, peeled, and sliced
1 teaspoon cinnamon
1 cup chopped nuts
1 box yellow cake mix
1 (3-ounce) box instant vanilla pudding mix
½ cup salad oil
4 eggs
½ teaspoon vanilla
1½ cups shredded coconut
1 (12-ounce) can frozen coconut milk, thawed

Preheat oven to 350°F. Put butter in 9 x 13-inch pan and melt in oven. Pour melted butter in bowl. Place apples into pan. Lay flat. Pan should be filled half full. Sprinkle cinnamon over the apples. Sprinkle nuts. Pour melted butter all over.

Blend cake mix, pudding mix, salad oil, eggs, vanilla, and shredded coconut together. Add coconut milk. Pour mixture over apples in greased pan. Bake for 45 to 50 minutes.

PINK COCONUT MOCHI

Makes about 4 dozen

- 4 cups mochiko
- 2 cups sugar
- 3 tablespoons butter, melted and cooled
- 1 (12-ounce) can frozen coconut milk, thawed
- 2 cups water
- 1 tablespoon vanilla
- 2 to 3 drops red food color
- Katakuriko (potato starch) for sprinkling

Mix together mochiko, sugar, butter, milk, water, vanilla, and food color. Blend thoroughly until smooth. Pour into greased microwave tube pan. Cover with plastic wrap. Microwave on high for 15 minutes. If pan does not automatically rotate, rotate the pan after 8 minutes. Remove plastic wrap immediately, being careful of steam. Cool for 10 minutes or longer before removing mochi from pan onto board sprinkled with katakuriko. Cut into serving pieces with plastic knife. Roll in katakuriko.

BIBINGKA–STICKY RICE CAKE

Serves 9 to 16

Street vendors in the Philippines sell this cake steamed and wrapped in a banana leaf. This version is baked in a pan to make it easier to make at home. Vanilla and grated coconut adds texture and another layer of flavor.

- ¼ cup butter, melted
- 1 banana leaf (optional)
- 2 cups mochiko (sweet rice flour)
- 1 cup light brown sugar, packed
- 1 teaspoon vanilla
- ¼ teaspoon salt
- 2 teaspoons baking powder
- 3 eggs, beaten
- 1 (13.5-ounce) can coconut milk
- ¼ cup grated coconut

Preheat oven to 325°F. Butter 8-inch square or round baking pan, then line with banana leaf, if using, cut to dimensions of the pan. In a bowl, combine all ingredients except grated coconut; mix 1 to 2 minutes or until well-blended. Pour into prepared pan and sprinkle grated coconut on top. Bake 1 hour or until a toothpick inserted in center comes out clean.

CRISPY COCONUT COOKIES

Makes about 4 dozen

Cookies make great gifts and tend to ship well. Crispy cookies, however, need to be packed very well to avoid crumbling. These cookies also make great hostess gifts.

1 cup butter or margarine
1 cup sugar
1½ teaspoons vanilla extract
2 cups flour
1½ cups shredded coconut

Preheat oven to 350°F. In large mixing bowl, cream butter and sugar until light and fluffy. Add vanilla extract; beat thoroughly. Mix in flour; add coconut and mix well. Shape into walnut-size balls and place on ungreased baking sheets; flatten with bottom of a glass dipped in flour. Bake for 20 to 25 minutes or until golden brown.

Cool completely and store in airtight container at room temperature.

COCONUT-MACADAMIA NUT COOKIES

Makes 4½ dozen

- 1 cup butter or margarine, softened
- 1 cup brown sugar, packed
- ½ cup sugar
- 1 egg
- 2¼ cups flour
- 1 teaspoon baking soda
- 1 cup flaked coconut
- 3½ ounces macadamia nuts, coarsely chopped

Preheat oven to 375°F. Mix butter, sugars, and egg. Stir in flour and baking soda (dough will be stiff). Stir in coconut and nuts. Drop dough by heaping teaspoonfuls about 2-inches apart onto ungreased cookie sheet. Bake for 8 to 10 minutes or until light brown. (Centers will be soft.)

Cool slightly, remove from cookie sheet.

COCONUT WASHBOARDS

Makes about 20

A popular cookie in the 1920s and 1930s and still popular today in some areas of the country, "washboards" got their name from the ridges made by pressing a fork into the dough before baking.

- ½ cup unsalted butter, softened
- 1 cup light brown sugar, firmly packed
- 1 teaspoon vanilla
- ¼ teaspoon coconut extract
- 1 large whole egg
- 1 large egg yolk
- 2 cups unbleached flour
- ¾ teaspoon double-acting baking powder
- ¼ teaspoon baking soda
- Pinch of salt
- 1 cup sweetened coconut flakes, packed

In a bowl, cream together butter and brown sugar until light; beat in vanilla, coconut extract, whole egg, and egg yolk. In another bowl, sift together flour, baking powder, baking soda, and salt. Stir the flour mixture into the butter mixture; stir in the coconut; cover and chill the dough for 20 minutes or until firm.

Preheat oven to 375°F. Spoon slightly rounded tablespoons of dough into floured palm of hand and form into 2½ inch long logs. Place logs 3 inches apart on greased baking sheets. Using a fork dipped in flour, press the back of the tines lengthwise into the logs, flattening them to 4 inches long and 1½ inches wide. (The marks from the tines of the fork should all be lengthwise.) Bake for 10 to 12 minutes or until they are golden around the edges.

Cool on baking sheets for 5 minutes then transfer the cookies to racks and cool completely.

SKY HIGH COCONUT CREAM PIE

Serves 8

The garden setting of the Willows restaurant on O'ahu was legendary, and so was this pie, known for its tall, billowing topping of meringue.

2 cups milk
½ cup sugar
¼ cup grated fresh coconut
5 tablespoons cornstarch
4 egg yolks
1 tablespoon butter
Pinch of salt
Vanilla extract, to taste

1 (9-inch) pie shell, baked

MERINGUE

4 to 6 egg whites
Approximately 1 tablespoon sugar for each egg white
Grated fresh coconut

Put milk, sugar, and coconut in saucepan over medium heat and cook until it comes to near boil; mix cornstarch and egg yolks together with a little water and add to milk mixture, stirring continually until thickened over low heat. Add butter, salt, and vanilla. Stir, cool, and pour into baked and cooled pie shell. Top with meringue.

To prepare meringue, beat egg whites until stiff but not dry; add sugar gradually, beating continuously. Spread over cooled filling, sealing to edges of pastry. Sprinkle coconut over top. Brown in 400°F oven.

DOUBLE-CRUSTED COCONUT PIE

Serves 8

There was a time when the double crust coconut pie, filled with grated fresh coconut, was popular. While shredded coconut is commonly found at the grocer's today, in the old days, one had to husk and grate the coconut oneself.

Pastry for 2-crust pie
6 cups shredded coconut
⅔ cup sugar
¼ teaspoon salt
1 cup coconut milk
3 egg whites
Milk

Preheat oven to 400°F. Line 9-inch pie pan with pastry. In medium bowl, combine coconut, sugar, salt, and coconut milk. In small mixing bowl, beat egg whites until stiff peaks form. Gently fold meringue into coconut mixture; pour into pastry lined pie pan; cover with top crust and flute edges. Brush crust lightly with milk. Bake for 30 minutes or until crust is golden.

HAUPIA

Serves 16 to 24

⅓ cup cornstarch
½ cup sugar
⅛ teaspoon salt
2 (12-ounce) cans coconut milk, divided use

Combine cornstarch, sugar, and salt. Stir in ½ cup of the coconut milk; blend to form smooth paste.

In a pot, heat remaining coconut milk; bring to a boil. Add cornstarch mixture. Cook, stirring frequently for about 20 minutes or until thickened. Pour into 8 x 8-inch pan. Cool and refrigerate. Cut into 1½-inch squares.

HAUPIA CREAM CHEESE PIE

Serves 18 to 24

CRUST

2 cups (about 24 crackers) crushed graham crackers
1 cup (2 blocks) butter, melted

CREAM CHEESE FILLING

2 (8-ounce) packages cream cheese, softened
1½ cups powdered sugar, sifted
1 teaspoon vanilla
2 cups Cool Whip

HAUPIA

3 (12-ounce) cans coconut milk
1¼ cups sugar
1¼ cups cornstarch

To make the crust, grind or crush graham crackers into crumbs. Mix with melted butter and press into 9 x 13-inch pan. Refrigerate.

To make the filling, beat cream cheese and sugar; add vanilla. Stir in Cool Whip. Spread on crust. Refrigerate until set.

To make the haupia, in a saucepan, mix all ingredients until smooth.

Cook on medium heat, stirring continuously, until mixture thickens. Remove from heat and cool down mixture, continuing to stir. When cool to touch, pour haupia over cream cheese filling.

Refrigerate pie to set.

HAUPIA CHOCOLATE PIE

Serves 18 to 24

CRUST

2 cups graham crackers, crushed (about 24 crackers)
1 cup butter, melted

HAUPIA

3 (12-ounce) cans frozen coconut milk, thawed
1¼ cups sugar
1¼ cups cornstarch

CHOCOLATE TOPPING

3 boxes cook-and-serve chocolate pudding
4½ cups milk

To make crust, grind or crush graham crackers into crumbs. Mix with melted butter and press into 9 x 13-inch pan. Refrigerate.

To make haupia, in a pot, mix all haupia ingredients until smooth. Cook on medium heat, stirring continuously until mixture thickens. Spread over crust. Refrigerate.

To make chocolate topping, combine pudding mix and milk; cook on medium heat, stirring continuously until thick and bubbles appear. Remove from heat and cool slightly while continuing to mix so "skin" doesn't form. Spread pudding over haupia. Refrigerate.

OKINAWAN SWEET POTATO HAUPIA SQUARES WITH MACADAMIA SHORTBREAD CRUST

Serves 18 to 24

Everyone in Hawai'i has their version of this popular dessert. Frank Abraham, host of Cooking Hawaiian Style, shares his mom's version made with a buttery macadamia nut crust, then a purple sweet potato layer topped with a layer of haupia.

MACADAMIA NUT CRUST

1½ cups flour
⅛ teaspoon salt
½ cup butter, at room temperature
¼ cup sugar
1 cup chopped unsalted macadamia nuts
1 large egg yolk

SWEET POTATO FILLING

2 pounds Okinawan or Moloka'i sweet potato, boiled and peeled
½ cup sugar
1 (8-ounce) block cream cheese, softened
Pinch of salt
¼ cup milk

HAUPIA TOPPING

2 (13.5-ounce) cans coconut milk, divided
⅓ cup cornstarch
Pinch of salt
½ cup sugar

GARNISH

¼ cup chopped macadamia nuts or shredded coconut

Preheat oven to 350°F. Line a 9 x 13 x 2-inch baking pan with parchment paper. Using a chopping blade, process the flour and salt until well-combined. Add the butter and sugar; pulse until mixture is well-combined and crumbly. Add nuts and egg yolk and pulse again until mixture is moistened. Press the mixture lightly into prepared baking pan. Bake for 20 to 25 minutes or until golden brown; cool.

Mash sweet potatoes while still hot. Add sugar, cream cheese, salt, and milk. Mix gently until well-combined, but do not overmix. Spread the sweet potato filling over macadamia nut crust. Place in the refrigerator while preparing the Haupia Topping.

Mix ¼ cup of coconut milk with cornstarch; set aside. In a 3-quart saucepan, combine the remaining coconut milk, salt, and sugar over medium heat. Bring to a boil. Stirring constantly, add the cornstarch slurry and cook until haupia starts to thicken. Boil for one minute. Remove from heat. Cover saucepan with lid to prevent skin from forming; cool to room temperature. Pour haupia onto sweet potato filling and sprinkle with macadamia nuts or shredded coconut to garnish. Chill for about 2 hours or until haupia is firm. Cut into bars to serve.

COCONUT CUSTARD PIE

Serves 8

You can make your own pie shell or take a shortcut with a purchased one from the supermarket. The coconut flakes will rise to the top, creating a coarse texture on the top surface. Coconut lovers, enjoy!

1 (9-inch) unbaked pie shell

FILLING
2 cups beaten eggs (about 8 large eggs)
1 cup sugar
½ teaspoon salt
½ tablespoon vanilla
4 cups milk
1 teaspoon nutmeg
1½ cups coconut flakes

Preheat oven to 300°F. Beat the eggs lightly; add the rest of the ingredients and mix well.

Pour into the pie shell and bake for about 1 hour. Cool before serving.

HAUPIA MAC NUT DESSERT

Serves 18 to 24

1 cup butter or margarine
1 cup sugar, divided use
2 cups flour
½ cup chopped macadamia nuts
½ cup cornstarch
2¾ cups water
2 (12-ounce) cans frozen coconut milk, thawed

GARNISH

1 (8-ounce) container frozen whipped topping, thawed
½ cup shredded coconut

Preheat oven to 350°F. Cream butter with ⅓ cup of the sugar in large mixing bowl. Mix in flour and nuts. Press evenly into a 9 x 13-inch baking pan. Bake for 15 to 18 minutes; cool.

Combine the remaining ⅔ cup sugar with the cornstarch in a saucepan, stir in water and coconut milk. Cook over low heat, stirring constantly, until thickened.

Cool and pour over baked crust; refrigerate to chill thoroughly. Garnish with whipped topping and shredded coconut before servings.

COCONUT BREAD PUDDING

Serves 18 to 24

3 eggs
¾ cup granulated sugar
4 cups milk
6 tablespoons coconut milk
8 cups diced bread (about ½-inch cubes)
½ cup chopped toasted macadamia nuts
½ cup toasted coconut flakes

GARNISH (PER SERVING)

2 tablespoons coconut syrup
Whipped cream
Pineapple, diced
Toasted macadamia nuts, chopped
Toasted coconut flakes

Preheat oven to 325°F. Whisk eggs and sugar together. Add milk and coconut milk, and mix thoroughly.

Layer bread, macadamia nuts, and coconut flakes in 9 x 13-inch pan. Pour custard mixture evenly over top and let custard soak into bread. Bake for 45 minutes to 1 hour, until a toothpick inserted into the center comes out clean.

When serving, drizzle about 2 tablespoons of coconut syrup over each portion. Top with a swirl of whipped cream. Sprinkle with diced pineapple, macadamia nuts, and coconut flakes.

HALO HALO POPSICLES

This recipe comes from Frank Abraham, host of Cooking Hawaiian Style.

UBE LAYER

½ cup frozen grated ube or Okinawan sweet potato
½ cup heavy cream
¼ cup milk
¼ teaspoon vanilla extract
¼ cup sugar

FRUIT LAYER

1 cup unsweetened coconut milk
4 tablespoons sugar
¾ cup diced mango, coconut gelatin, jackfruit, macapuno, or lychee

Place the ube, cream, milk, vanilla, and sugar in small saucepan over medium heat and whisk until the sugar has dissolved. Remove from heat and put mixture into a blender. Blend until smooth. Use caution when blending as the steam and heat need to escape.

Divide the mixture between the popsicle molds, filling them halfway. Place in the freezer for about 2 hours and ensure that the first layer is at least semi-frozen before proceeding.

When the frozen ube layer is ready, prepare the fruit layer. Place the coconut milk in a small bowl and add 4 tablespoons sugar. Whisk until the mixture is smooth and the sugar has dissolved. Stir in your favorite fruit and set aside.

Remove the molds from the freezer and evenly divide the mixture between the molds. Insert the sticks and freeze until completely frozen for 4 to 6 hours.

RECIPE CREDITS

from *Aloha Cuisine* by Sam Choy
- Baked Coconut Taro
- Baked Sweet Potatoes
- Coconut Bread Pudding
- Coconut Mac-Nut Shrimp with Guava Sweet & Sour Sauce
- Ginger Pesto-Crusted ʻŌpakapaka with Coconut Cream Sauce
- Tahitian Crabmeat Soup

from *Aunty Audrey's Big Island Eats* by Audrey Wilson
- Chicken Satay with Peanut Sauce
- Hilo Huli Mushroom Soup
- Squid Lūʻau

from *The Best of the Best Hawaiʻi Local Desserts* by Jean Hee
- Coconut-Macadamia Nut Cookies
- Coconut-Pineapple Cream Cake
- Curried Lobster with Fried Haupia
- Haupia
- Haupia Chocolate Pie
- Haupia Cream Cheese Pie
- Yummy Coconut Apple Cake

from *Celebrating in Hawaiʻi* by Muriel Miura
- Haupia Mac Nut Dessert
- Hawaiian Shrimp Curry

from *The Choy of Seafood* by Sam Choy
- Seared Albacore Tuna with Coconut-Ginger Sauce
- Tropical Island Poke

from *Cooking Hawaiian Style* by Lanai Tabura and Frank Abraham
- Chef Ippy Aiona's Pork Belly Adobo

Kālua Lūʻau Lasagna Rolls with Haupia Béchamel Sauce
Melveen Leed's Crustacean Polynesia

from *Cooking Hawaiian Style Two* by Lanai Tabura and Frank Abraham
Chef Lee Anne Wong's Dumplings with Lemongrass Broth
Chicken Panang with Macadamia Nuts
Coconut Shrimp
Halo Halo Popsicles
Maile Symmond's Evil Princess
Okinawan Sweet Potato Haupia Squares with Macadamia Shortbread Crust

from *A Filipino Kitchen* by Adam Tabura
Arroz Valenciana (Paella)
Bibingka–Sticky Rice Cake
Bicol Express–Spicy Pork Belly in Coconut Milk
Chicken Afritada

from *Hawaiʻi Bakes* edited by Mona Taga and Galyn Wong
Piña Colada Pound Cake

from *Hawaiʻi's Best Mochi Recipes* by Jean Watanabe Hee
Pink Coconut Mochi

from *Hawaiʻi's Favorite Pineapple Recipes* by Joannie Dobbs and Betty Shimabukuro
Coconut Thai Rice

from *Poke Hawaiʻi's Food* by Sam Choy
Simply ʻAhi Ceviche

from *Sam Choy's Kitchen* by Sam Choy

South Pacific Coconut Rice with Sautéed Pork Loin
Sweet Potato Coconut Casserole

from *Sam Choy's Sampler* by Sam Choy
Papaya, Mint, and Coconut Soup

from *What Big Island Likes to Eat* by Audrey Wilson
Coconut Cream of Celery Soup

from *What Hawai'i Likes to Eat* by Muriel Miura and Betty Shimabukuro
Coconut Washboards
Curried Mahimahi
Sky High Coconut Cream Pie

from *What Hawai'i Likes to Eat Hana Hou* by Muriel Miura and Galyn Wong
Crispy Coconut Cookies
Double-Crusted Coconut Pie

from *What Maui Likes to Eat* by Tylun Pang
Coconut-Curry Haleakalā Ranch Lamb Chops with Mango Salsa
Coconut Custard Pie

PHOTO CREDITS

Adobe Firefly: pages 58, 60, 89, 93

Dreamstime.com: cover, pages 47, 84, 107

Leigh Anne Meeks: pages 14, 22, 41, 45, 51, 71, 103, 109

Douglas Peebles: pages 9, 11, 13, 27, 31, 33, 66

Kaz Tanabe: pages 36, 52, 69, 77, 87, 95, 97